1/06

# SPIDERS SET II

# FUNNEL-WEB SPIDERS

Jill C. Wheeler
ABDO Publishing Company

# visit us at
# www.abdopub.com

Published by ABDO Publishing Company, 4940 Viking Drive, Edina, Minnesota 55435. Copyright © 2006 by Abdo Consulting Group, Inc. International copyrights reserved in all countries. No part of this book may be reproduced in any form without written permission from the publisher. The Checkerboard Library™ is a trademark and logo of ABDO Publishing Company.

Printed in the United States.

Cover Photo: Peter Arnold
Interior Photos: Animals Animals pp. 11, 13; Corbis pp. 7, 17; CSIRO pp. 5, 9; Dr. J White p. 19; Peter Arnold p. 21; SuperStock p. 15

Series Coordinator: Stephanie Hedlund
Editors: Heidi M. Dahmes, Stephanie Hedlund
Art Direction: Neil Klinepier

## Library of Congress Cataloging-in-Publication Data

Wheeler, Jill C., 1964-
    Funnel-web spiders / Jill C. Wheeler.
       p. cm. -- (Spiders. Set II)
    Includes bibliographical references.
    ISBN 1-59679-294-9
     1. Agelenidae--Juvenile literature.  I. Title.

    QL458.42.A3W43 2006
    595.4'4--dc22

                                                    2005045733

# CONTENTS

# FUNNEL-WEB SPIDERS

In the animal kingdom, there is a group of animals called **arthropods**. Members of this group have skeletons on the outside of their bodies. **Arachnids** are part of this group. Scorpions, ticks, and mites are arachnids. All spiders are, too.

There are about 100 spider **families** in the world. Funnel-web spiders are in the Dipluridae family. Scientists have identified at least 250 different species of this spider.

Funnel-web spiders have a **venom** that is **neurotoxic**. It is deadly to most of this spider's prey. It is also **dangerous** for humans. So, it is important to be able to identify a funnel-web spider. That way you can avoid being bitten.

*A funnel-web spider's venom is more harmful to insects than to mammals. So, researchers are working to take parts of this venom and make natural insecticides, or poisons to kill insects.*

# SIZES

Funnel-web spiders can be small or large. The largest species can grow to be one and one-quarter inch (3.2 cm) long. The smallest funnel-web spiders are only about one-quarter inch (6 mm) long. Females are usually bigger than males.

Females spend most of their lives tucked away in cozy burrows. They rarely go more than a few feet away from their homes. Some female funnel-web spiders can live for up to 20 years.

Funnel-web spiders are fully grown after about three years. Male funnel-web spiders leave their burrows when they are mature and ready to mate. Males only live for six to nine months after they leave. So, their life span is only three to four years.

A few species of funnel-web spiders are known for their large fangs.

# SHAPES

Funnel-web spiders look like many other spiders. They have eight long legs. They also have a **cephalothorax** and an **abdomen**.

All funnel-web spiders have two **pedipalps** and two **chelicerae**. These leglike organs are found at the front of the cephalothorax.

There are several features that set a funnel-web spider apart from other spiders. One is the flat top on its cephalothorax. This is called a carapace. It acts as a hard, protective covering.

Other features include **spinnerets** and spurs. The fingerlike spinnerets are visible at the end of the funnel-web spider's abdomen. Male funnel-web spiders often have a spur, or swelling, along their second leg. They use this spur during mating.

# The Body Parts of a Funnel-Web Spider

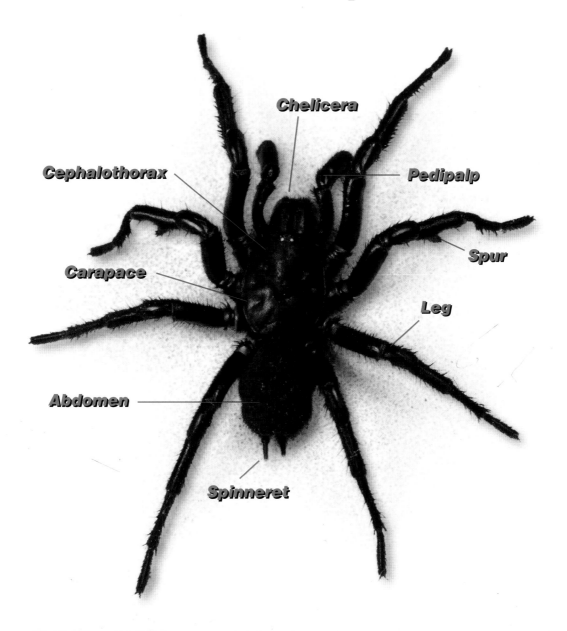

Chelicera

Cephalothorax

Pedipalp

Spur

Carapace

Leg

Abdomen

Spinneret

# COLORS

Funnel-web spiders are dark-colored spiders. But, the colors vary. Some funnel-webs are black. Others are dark plum, reddish brown, or brown.

Short hairs cover the bodies and long legs of funnel-web spiders. The carapace is always glossy with few hairs. These things can make the spider look very dark.

The funnel-web spider's coloring helps it blend into its surroundings. These spiders need to avoid the sun to stay alive. So, they stay in their dark, moist burrows during the day. They hunt at night. This often makes it difficult to find the funnel-web spider.

**Opposite page:** *Most male funnel-webs hide from the sun under boards or rocks. But, they can be seen during the day if their shelter is bothered.*

# WHERE THEY LIVE

Most funnel-web spiders live in tropical and subtropical areas. They are found in parts of North America, Africa, Asia, and Australia.

Funnel-web spiders get their name from the webs they build. Outside the burrow is a flat web of silk with a funnel-shaped entrance. The entrance leads to the heart of the burrow.

Most funnel-web spiders live in burrows that are less than 12 inches (30 cm) underground. They build these burrows in cool places. Their favorite spots are under rocks and logs.

Near cities, funnel-web spiders live in gardens and under thick shrubs. A few species live in trees. They make their homes in holes and cracks in tree trunks and branches.

Only male funnel-web spiders wander away from their homes. They may crawl into houses, sheds, garages, or swimming pools. They can end up in someone's shoe or clothes left on the floor. That is usually when humans see them.

# SENSES

Funnel-web spiders may have six or eight eyes. The number of eyes depends on the species. But, the eyes of all funnel-web spiders are grouped close together. Like most spiders, funnel-webs do not have good eyesight.

A funnel-web spider is most active at night. Because of the darkness, it does not rely on sight for hunting. Instead, it relies on its ability to sense vibrations.

All animals create vibrations when they move. The hairs on the funnel-web's body and legs act as sensors for these vibrations. This spider also uses the silken entrance to its burrow to sense vibrations.

The funnel-web's burrow entrance has silk strands that stretch out and work like trip wires. Any creature that touches the silk sends vibrations to the center of the web. The spider senses these vibrations and is alerted to anything that is approaching.

**Opposite page: *Hairs on the funnel-web spider's body and legs are highly sensitive to vibrations.***

# DEFENSE

Funnel-web spiders use their senses to avoid **predators**. They have to defend themselves against large centipedes and king crickets that venture into their burrows. Birds, lizards, and some small mammals also like to eat funnel-web spiders.

The funnel-web spider's first defense is to hide. If that doesn't work, the spider will fight. A funnel-web will rear up on its back legs and show its fangs. If still attacked, drops of **venom** will appear. And, the spider will snap its head like it is stabbing a victim.

The **neurotoxic** venom of the funnel-web spider is deadly to insects and humans. However, it is not deadly to most other mammals.

The Sydney funnel-web spider is the most well-known species in Australia. The male Sydney funnel-web's venom is five times stronger than the female's venom. If not treated, a bite can kill a human in as little as 15 minutes.

Before 1981, bites from the male Sydney funnel-web spider killed 13 people. Then, researchers created an **antivenin**. No one has died from a funnel-web spider's bite since then.

*Funnel-web spiders cannot jump or chase after king crickets or their other enemies. Hiding and fighting are the only ways funnel-webs can keep attackers away.*

# FOOD

Funnel-web spiders mainly eat insects such as beetles and cockroaches. Some species of funnel-web spiders also eat small reptiles or tree frogs.

Typically, a funnel-web spider will wait until something hits a trip wire in its web. Then, the spider races out of its burrow to the invader. The spider rears up on its back legs and shows its fangs. Next, it thrusts down quickly and sinks its fangs into its victim.

The funnel-web's fangs **inject** deadly **venom** into the prey. The venom quickly makes the spider's victim unable to move. When possible, the spider drags its prey back into the burrow to eat.

Like other spiders, funnel-webs inject juices into their food. These juices break down the food so the spider can absorb it.

*A funnel-web spider that is ready to attack*

# BABIES

Funnel-web spiders have interesting mating habits. Both males and females like to fight. The male uses his spurs to keep the female from biting him.

After mating, the female spins an egg sac of silk. She carefully puts more than 100 eggs into the sac. Once wrapped, the eggs are tough and shaped like disks. The mother then puts the egg sac safely in the back of her burrow.

The female funnel-web cleans and turns the egg sac while the eggs are **incubating** in the burrow. She is always ready to defend her eggs against **predators**.

The eggs hatch after about three weeks. The babies, or spiderlings, stay in their mother's burrow for several months. They shed their skeletons twice during their stay. This is called molting.

After their second molt, spiderlings leave their mother's burrow. Then, they strike out to make their own burrows and begin the cycle again.

*Molting is a multistep process. First, a spider hangs from a silk strand. During this time, its new skeleton is growing. Then, the spider moves until the old skeleton breaks open. Finally, the spider withdraws its legs from the old skeleton and stretches them. The spider now leaves the old skeleton behind.*

# GLOSSARY

**abdomen** - the rear body part of an arthropod.

**antivenin** - a kind of medicine used to reverse the effects of a poisonous spider bite.

**arachnid** (uh-RAK-nuhd) - an order of animals with two body parts and eight legs.

**arthropod** - a member of the phylum Arthropoda with an exterior skeleton.

**cephalothorax** (seh-fuh-luh-THAWR-aks) - the front body part of an arachnid that has the head and thorax.

**chelicera** (kih-LIH-suh-ruh) - either of the leglike organs of a spider that has a fang attached to it.

**dangerous** - able or likely to cause injury or harm.

**family** - a group that scientists use to classify similar plants or animals. It ranks above a genus and below an order.

**incubate** - to keep eggs warm so that they will hatch.

**inject** - to forcefully introduce a fluid into the body, usually with a needle or something sharp.

**neurotoxic** - harmful to the nervous system of the body.

**pedipalp** (PEH-duh-palp) - either of the leglike organs of a spider that are used to sense motion and catch prey.

**predator** - an animal that kills and eats other animals.

**spinneret** - either of the two body parts attached to the abdomen of a spider where the silk is made.

**venom** - a poison produced by some animals and insects. It usually enters a victim through a bite or sting.

# WEB SITES

To learn more about funnel-web spiders, visit ABDO Publishing Company on the World Wide Web at **www.abdopub.com**. Web sites about these spiders are featured on our Book Links page. These links are routinely monitored and updated to provide the most current information available.

# INDEX